WILD BUILDINGS AND BRIDGES

˭ARCHITECTURE INSPIRED BY NATURE˭

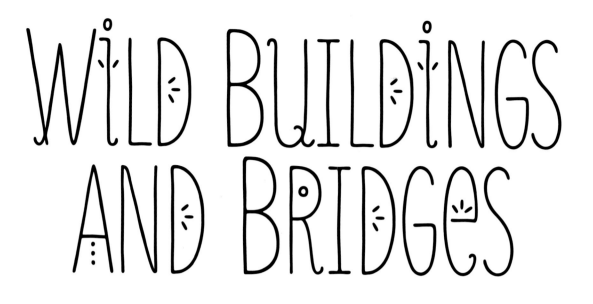

ETTA KANER · CARL WIENS

KIDS CAN PRESS

For David, a fellow lover of nature — E.K.
To my father, who showed me how to build things — C.W.

Acknowledgments

I am extremely grateful to Gretchen Hooker, Project Manager, Education Resources of Biomimicry Institute, for her patience, persistence, diligence and generosity of time and thought. Special thanks to my editors Stacey Roderick and Katie Scott, designer Marie Bartholomew and illustrator Carl Wiens for their creativity and insight.

Photo Credits

Page 11: Health Sciences Education Building and Biomedical Sciences Partnership Building at Phoenix Biomedical Campus, Phoenix, AZ, designed by CO Architects with Ayers Saint Gross. © Bill Timmerman. Page 13: The "Gherkin." © CEphoto, Uwe Aranas. Page 14: Council House 2. © deadlyphoto.com / Alamy Stock Photo. Page 18: The Heliotrope. © WENN Ltd. / Alamy Stock Photo. Page 23: Técnico Chixot Education Center. © Genevieve Croker, Long Way Home. Page 26: Guggenheim Museum. © Tony Hisgett.

Text © 2018 Etta Kaner
Illustrations © 2018 Carl Wiens

Kids Can Press gratefully acknowledges the financial support of the Government of Ontario, through the Ontario Media Development Corporation; the Ontario Arts Council; the Canada Council for the Arts; and the Government of Canada, through the CBF, for our publishing activity.

Many of the designations used by manufacturers and sellers to distinguish their products are claimed as trademarks. Where those designations appear in this book and Kids Can Press Ltd. was aware of a trademark claim, the designations have been printed in initial capital letters (e.g., Bristol board).

Neither the Publisher nor the Author shall be liable for any damage that may be caused or sustained as a result of conducting any of the activities in this book without specifically following instructions, conducting the activities without proper supervision or ignoring the cautions contained in the book.

Published in Canada and the U.S. by Kids Can Press Ltd.
25 Dockside Drive, Toronto, ON M5A 0B5

Kids Can Press is a Corus Entertainment Inc. company

www.kidscanpress.com

The artwork in this book was hand drawn and rendered in Adobe Illustrator.
The text is set in Avenir LT Std.

Edited by Stacey Roderick and Katie Scott
Designed by Marie Bartholomew

Printed and bound in Shenzhen, China, in 3/2018 by C & C Offset

MIX
Paper from responsible sources
FSC® C008047

CM 18 0 9 8 7 6 5 4 3 2 1

Library and Archives Canada Cataloguing in Publication

Kaner, Etta, author
Wild buildings and bridges : architecture inspired by nature / Etta Kaner ; illustrated by Carl Wiens.

Includes bibliographical references and index.
ISBN 978-1-77138-781-1 (hardcover)

1. Architecture — Environmental aspects — Juvenile literature. 2. Building — Environmental aspects — Juvenile literature. I. Wiens, Carl, illustrator II. Title.

NA2542.35.K36 2018   j720'.47   C2017-906759-1

CONTENTS

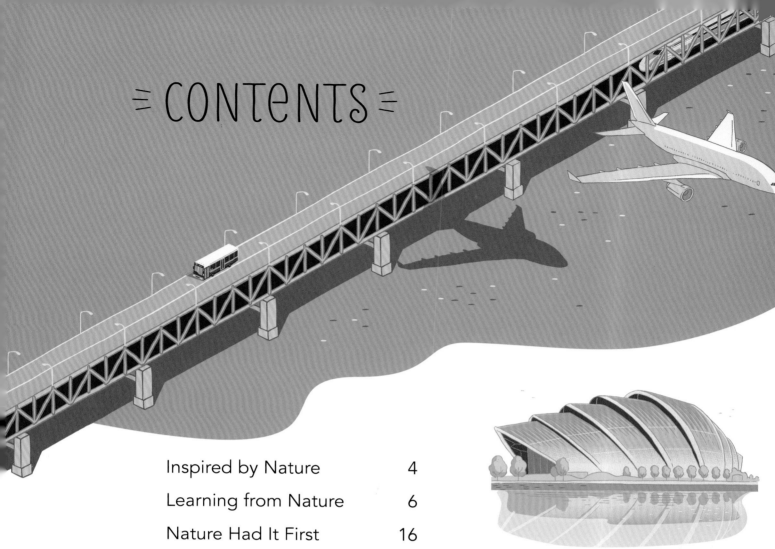

Inspired by Nature

What comes to mind when you hear the word *nature*? Trees and grass? Birds and insects? Do you think of buildings or bridges? Probably not. After all, they are structures made by people, using concrete and steel to make straight lines and sharp corners. Well, you might be surprised to find out that there *can* be a strong link between nature and built structures.

As a matter of fact, many architects look to nature to help them solve their building challenges. And they've found some incredible solutions, including a cactus-inspired way to cool a building without using a lot of energy and an earthquake-proof bridge design based on the roots of a special type of grass!

Some architects have come up with design solutions, only to discover that they are similar to what also works in nature. For example, to deal with potential flooding, buildings and whole communities have been designed to float on water, much like some water plants do.

Architects might also think about the *laws* of nature when they design a structure. These laws are the rules that nature always follows. For example, nature recycles, never wastes material and is full of curves and patterns. You'll find some unbelievable structures that also follow some of these laws!

Nature's beauty also inspires architects. Would you believe there is a museum that moves like a bird? Or a house built in the shape of a feathered snake?

In this book, you'll meet some ingenious architects and designers who have been inspired by nature to design wild and wonderful buildings and bridges. And be sure to check out the cool experiments as well as try your hand at designing your own buildings and bridges — inspired by nature, of course!

= Learning From Nature =

Do you think animals and plants can hold the secret to designing a building or a bridge? They definitely can! Many architects look to the natural world to help them with their building challenges because they realize that nature has a better way of doing things — often without using up a whole lot of resources. This approach to architecture is called biomimetic, from the ancient Greek words *bios*, meaning life, and *mimesis*, meaning to imitate. Take a look …

WETLAND COPYCATS

Imagine you're visiting a wetland. You might see dragonflies, reeds, water lilies, ducks, frogs and herons. What you might *not* see is what's below the surface of the water: the living and rotting plants in sticky black muck. Sounds gross? It's this gross part that inspired the invention of the Living Machine — a system used by some buildings in North America to clean and save water.

The creators of the Living Machine knew that wetlands act like a filter to clean dirty water. When pollutants such as acid rain, fertilizers and animal poop enter the wetlands, some are absorbed by plants. The rest drop to the bottom, where bacteria gobble them up. Water that flows out of wetlands is much cleaner than when it entered.

The Living Machine works in the same way. It is a series of large tubs or tanks containing plants, snails, clams, algae and bacteria submerged in water. Dirty water from sinks and toilets in a building is piped down to slowly flow through the tanks. The organisms have a feast. By the time they're done, the water is clean enough to be used again for watering gardens, washing cars or filling toilets.

Wild Idea!

Scientists have invented a paint that mimics the way butterfly wings and some plant leaves are able to stay clean. The paint's rough texture forces rain droplets to keep a spherical (round) shape so that rainwater rolls right off, taking dirt particles with it. Scientists call this the lotus effect because it's how lotus leaves stay clean in muddy ponds. Just think how much tap water this paint saves when it comes to cleaning the outside of a large house!

The Living Machine

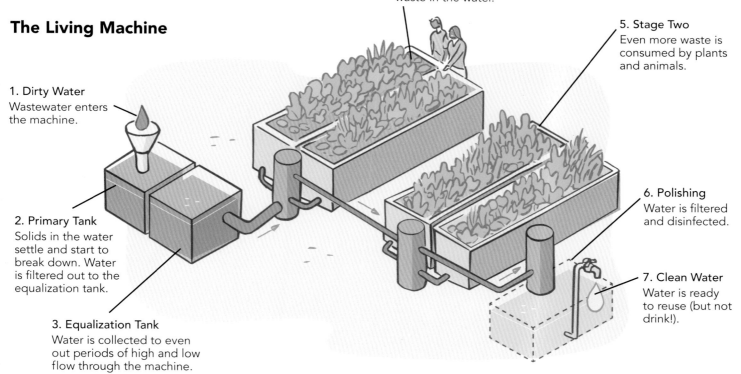

1. **Dirty Water**
Wastewater enters the machine.

2. **Primary Tank**
Solids in the water settle and start to break down. Water is filtered out to the equalization tank.

3. **Equalization Tank**
Water is collected to even out periods of high and low flow through the machine.

4. **Stage One**
Plants and animals consume waste in the water.

5. **Stage Two**
Even more waste is consumed by plants and animals.

6. **Polishing**
Water is filtered and disinfected.

7. **Clean Water**
Water is ready to reuse (but not drink!).

Turning the Desert Green

If you were given the job of building in the desert, one of your biggest design challenges would be dealing with the lack of available water — not just for drinking or washing but also for growing food. But thanks to inspiration from the Namibian fog-basking beetle, a clever designer has figured out a way to turn a part of the desert green.

Even though this beetle lives in the Namib Desert on the southwest coast of Africa, it has no problem getting fresh drinking water. During the day, the beetle hides deep under the sand. When it emerges after dark, its body is slightly cooler than the surrounding night air. As a foggy breeze blows in from the nearby sea, droplets of water form on its back. (A similar thing happens on your cooler bathroom mirror when you run a steamy hot shower.) To get a drink, the beetle simply tips its body forward, and water droplets run down its back into its mouth!

By mimicking this beetle, Seawater Greenhouses are able to produce fresh water in the desert — enough to grow veggies all year round as well as to supply water for crops outside. How? Warm, humid air is drawn through the greenhouse to a back wall covered with pipes filled with cool seawater. When the warm air hits the cool pipes, droplets of water form on their outsides and drip down into a holding tank.

Seawater Greenhouse

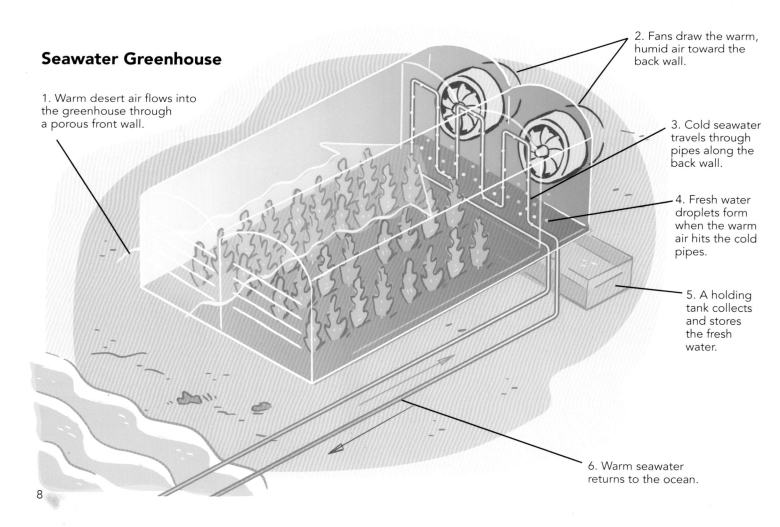

1. Warm desert air flows into the greenhouse through a porous front wall.

2. Fans draw the warm, humid air toward the back wall.

3. Cold seawater travels through pipes along the back wall.

4. Fresh water droplets form when the warm air hits the cold pipes.

5. A holding tank collects and stores the fresh water.

6. Warm seawater returns to the ocean.

The Wright Way

Frank Lloyd Wright is probably the most famous organic architect of all time. He believed that a building should make its site (the place where it's built) more beautiful. How? By using local materials and shapes that blend into the natural surroundings. For example, he believed a home in the desert should look very different from a home built in a forest. He wanted the buildings he designed to be in harmony with nature.

Wright's best-known house design, Fallingwater, is a good example of this idea. Located in a forest in southwestern Pennsylvania, the house is built over a waterfall and rushing stream. Large terraces (patios) mimic the pattern of rock ledges below the house, and its rough stone walls appear to be coming right out of the ground.

Wright also felt that natural light should be part of architecture. Buildings with many large windows would allow people to experience how light changes depending on the weather and the seasons. This was another way to bring people closer to nature in their daily lives.

The Wacky Way

Organic architect Javier Senosiain also thinks his structures should reflect nature. Many of his colorful buildings bring to mind serpents or amphibians. One such structure is an apartment building called the Quetzalcoatl Nest, named after a feathered Aztec snake god.

And as with many of Senosiain's designs, living in Quetzalcoatl feels a little like being inside a python. The rooms have curved walls, specially made sofas and tables molded out of the walls and beds carved into the walls. Would you want to live in one of Senosiain's creations?

Fallingwater in Mill Run, Pennsylvania, is a house that hangs over a waterfall. Architect: Frank Lloyd Wright.

A Moving Experience

Some organic architects are inspired by movement and changes they observe in nature.

Take Spanish architect Santiago Calatrava, for example. When he was asked to design the addition to the Milwaukee Art Museum, he was inspired by movements on the nearby lake — especially the soaring birds.

He designed a giant hall with an incredibly high glass ceiling and a movable sunscreen that looks like a giant bird about to take off. Although it weighs 81 tonnes (90 tons) and has the wingspan of a Boeing 747 airplane, the sunscreen can open or close in just three and a half minutes with barely a sound. Having also studied to be an engineer likely helped Calatrava accomplish this amazing design feat.

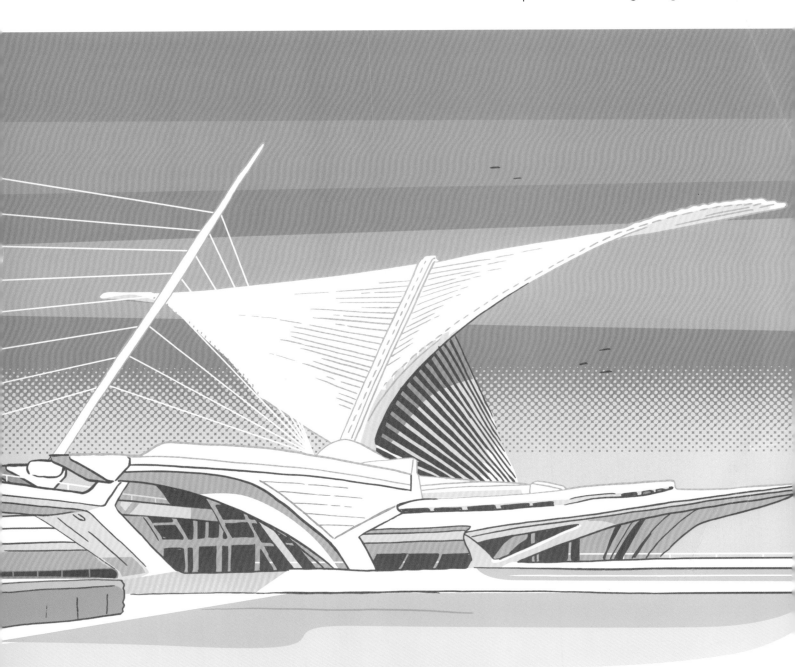

The top of the Milwaukee Art Museum in Milwaukee, Minnesota, looks like a giant bird. Architect: Santiago Calatrava.

While Calatrava has designed many buildings, he is probably most famous for his nature-inspired bridges.

It's easy to see the relationship the Puerto Bridge in northern Spain has to its natural surroundings. This arch bridge in the port of Ondarroa mimics the curves of the harbor that it crosses as well as the hills around the town. And if you look from afar at the riblike cables of the bridge with natural light flowing through them, you could very well be reminded of a fish skeleton.

The Puerto Bridge in Ondarroa, Spain, is used by both cars and pedestrians. Architect: Santiago Calatrava.

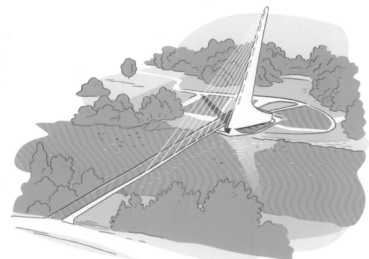

Many of Calatrava's bridges, like the Sundial Bridge in California, are built with a soaring mast and steel cables. The long sweeping lines of this bridge give the impression of movement, like the profile of a bird in flight. The really cool thing about this pedestrian bridge is that its mast acts as a giant sundial, casting a shadow that tells the time in a garden at the north end of the bridge.

The Sundial Bridge in Redding, California, is built without piers in order to protect the salmon spawning eggs in the Sacramento River below. Architect: Santiago Calatrava.

Wild Idea!

Some villagers in northeastern India weave bridges from the growing roots of rubber fig trees. The tree has a secondary root system above ground that can be trained to grow across rivers. Some bridges are more than one hundred years old!

= DESIGN TIME =

It's your turn to design your own building or bridge. For some inspiration, you might want to check out the list of some of nature's creations below. Use a pencil and paper to draw your design or ask your parents for permission to use a free online design program, such as Google SketchUp. Then let your imagination go wild!

Lotus flower: This beautiful flower comes in five colors: white, pink, red, blue and purple. It grows from the bottom of a muddy pond and yet blossoms on the surface of the water perfectly clean.

Agave desert plant: Because they grow in an arid (extremely dry) environment, agave plants need to collect as much water as possible. Channel-shaped leaves (that look something like a paper-towel roll cut in half lengthwise) catch and funnel any rain directly to the heart of the plant and its roots.

Armadillo: Armadillos are small mammals that have a protective bony shell made of keratin, the same material your fingernails are made of. The shell is made up of a number of bands that operate like hinges across its back. These bands allow the armadillo to curl up into a ball when threatened.

Mimic a Beetle!

Chances are you're not going to meet a Namibian beetle anytime soon, so why not try this activity to see how fog-basking works?

You'll need:

hot tap water

one ice cube

a short, wide-rimmed glass

a taller, narrow-rimmed glass

1. Pour the hot water into the shorter glass so that it is three-quarters full.

2. Place the tall glass upside down so that it sits inside the rim of the short glass.

3. Put the ice cube on top of the taller glass.

4. Watch what happens inside the tall glass for five minutes.

What happened?

As the hot water evaporates, the top glass will fill with water vapor. When the water vapor hits the cooler sides of the top glass, it collects into water droplets. This process is called condensation. As more water droplets come together to form larger drops, they become heavier and slide down the sides of the glass. Both the Namibian fog-basking beetle and the Seawater Greenhouse gather fresh water in this way.

It's Not Cool to Be Hot

Some architects have borrowed a trick or two from nature to make sure their buildings stay comfortably cool.

Terrific Trees

Have you ever heard of the urban heat-island effect? It's the term scientists use to describe how asphalt roads, parking lots, concrete buildings and sidewalks absorb the sun's heat during the day and then release it at night. This makes the air temperature in big cities several degrees warmer than surrounding rural areas. The extra heat can mean more need for air-conditioning, which in turn means higher energy use. It also increases the possibility of extreme weather conditions in that area.

One solution is to plant trees. Trees shade the concrete. They also cool the surrounding air when moisture evaporates from tiny holes on the underside of their leaves.

Inspired by this cooling feature of leaves, architects in Japan have designed a building that cools the air around it. The eastern facade, or outside wall, of the NBF Osaki Building is covered with porous pipes that run horizontally. (*Porous* means full of tiny holes.) Rainwater collected from the roof runs through these pipes. As sunlight heats the water, it evaporates through the little holes in the pipes and cools the air outside the building. A cooler outdoor temperature means that less energy is needed for inside air-conditioning. Just imagine how a whole city of these buildings could cool the urban environment!

Water evaporates from the porous pipes, cooling the air outside the NBF Osaki Building in Tokyo, Japan. Architects: Nikken Sekkei Ltd.

Vertical pleats on the saguaro cactus keep the stem shaded and cool.

As Cool as Canyons and Cactuses

Before designing the Health Sciences Education Building in Phoenix, Arizona, architects headed out to the surrounding Sonoran Desert. Why? To see how animals and plants adapted to the harsh climate, where summer daytime temperatures can reach as high as 48°C (118°F). Here's what they found.

Slot canyons: These deep, narrow passages wind through desert rock. Slot canyons block out direct sunlight and heat, making the bottom of the canyon much cooler than the open air — and a perfect place for animals to escape the desert heat.

Saguaro cactuses: These giant cactuses have vertical pleats or ridges (imagine the inside of corrugated cardboard) that create shade to protect the stem from the scorching desert sun.

The biomimetic Health Sciences Education Building in Phoenix, Arizona, was inspired by natural features found in the desert. Architects: CO Architects.

By combining these two desert features, the architects figured out how to beat the heat. The walls of a "canyon" running through the center of the six-story building provide shade but still allow natural light to filter in. The outside of the building has a pleated copper covering that reduces the direct sunlight hitting the building, similar to the way the ridges of the saguaro cactus protect it from the sun.

May the Strength Be with You

If you were designing a building or bridge, you'd probably think about how to make it strong and durable. Architects usually depend on materials such as concrete, steel and glass to do this. But sometimes they need a helping hand from nature to figure out the best way to use these materials.

The earthquake-resistant design of the Rion-Antirion Bridge in the Gulf of Corinth, Greece, features 200 steel pipes beneath each pier, mimicking the roots of vetiver grass (below). Architect: Berdj Mikaelian.

How to Survive an Earthquake ... as a Bridge

Building an almost 3.2 km (2 mi.) long bridge that stretches over a seabed in an active earthquake zone is not easy. It's even harder when there's nothing solid to build on — just hundreds of meters (or feet) of sand. That's the problem engineers faced when planning the Rion-Antirion Bridge over the Gulf of Corinth in Greece.

When wet sand is shaken (for example, by an earthquake), it turns to liquid. So setting bridge piers (supports) in wet sand was definitely going to be a challenge. Oddly enough, the solution they found was in the roots of grass — vetiver grass, to be specific.

These roots can grow as long as 7 m (23 ft.) and hold the soil of riverbanks in place so it doesn't wash away. Inspired by these roots, engineers took hollow steel pipes, each as tall as an eight-story building, and drove them down into the seabed beneath each pier location. Each set of 200 pipes was topped with gravel and a foundation before the pier was added. During an earthquake, the pipes actually stabilize the seabed sand and stop it from turning to liquid, keeping the bridge and the people on it safe. Incredible!

The Gherkin (Not the Eating Kind)

Architect Norman Foster's gherkin pickle–shaped building is world-famous. But it was actually inspired by a strange animal that lives at the bottom of the sea, not by the sour snack.

This animal, the Venus's flower-basket sponge, has no internal organs or brain — just a hollow, cylinder-shaped exoskeleton (outside skeleton) that has a lattice, or crisscross, pattern. The sponge's round shape and lattice pattern are made of many triangles to help give it strength to withstand the stress of underwater currents.

Looking to the sponge as a model, Foster designed the Gherkin's lattice pattern using thousands of glass triangles and diamond shapes set in a steel frame. Why triangles and diamonds? Triangles keep their form under force, which makes them the strongest shape. And diamonds are simply two triangles laid end to end. In addition, when many triangles are fitted together, they form a curve. Rounded sides on a building prevent the strong winds that often occur at the base of tall, straight-sided buildings and make it difficult for pedestrians to walk.

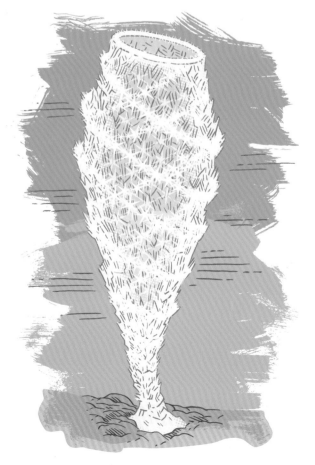

Known by many as "the Gherkin" because of its pickle shape, this building in London, England, was actually inspired by the Venus's flower-basket sponge (left). Architect: Norman Foster.

Saving on Energy

Architects who care about the environment design buildings that save energy. It's not always easy to figure out how to do this. But sometimes they find inspiration in the most unusual places!

Termite Towers to the Rescue!

If you traveled to southern Africa, you would see termite towers that can be as tall as three-story buildings. Inside of these towers, which are made of soil and termite spit and poop, are twisting tunnels. For many years, scientists believed that these tunnels helped keep termites cool by allowing naturally rising hot air to travel up through them and out the top of the tower. In fact, architect Mick Pearce was so inspired by the way he thought these towers worked that he used this system to design an energy-efficient office building in Melbourne, Australia.

The 10-story building is cooled when automatic shutters on one side of it open at night. This lets cool air into a space above the concrete ceilings that have been absorbing heat from the building throughout the day. The cool air chases out the warm air through vents. The cool air also gradually cools down the ceilings, making them ready to absorb heat again the next day.

The Council House 2 office building in Melbourne, Australia, was modeled on African termite towers (left). Architect: Mick Pearce.

Oops!

Scientists now believe that termite towers work more like lungs. Carbon dioxide is pushed outside through tiny holes in the outer walls, and oxygen enters the same way. Still, these architects have designed buildings that save a lot of energy and money on cooling. It looks like we can still learn from nature even when we don't completely understand how it works!

Stay Cool

When architects were asked to design a greenhouse for alpine plants, they had a major challenge: How could they recreate the cool, dry, windy conditions of a mountainous habitat in London, England? And how do you create these conditions without using energy-guzzling air conditioners and wind pumps? The answer was to mimic termite towers!

The Davies Alpine House is a greenhouse that is tall and narrow, like a termite tower. Deep under its floor is a concrete maze. The maze is naturally cool, just like a basement in a house, because it's below ground level. Air from the outside is drawn into the maze. As the air travels through the maze, it cools. This cooler air then flows through pipes and into the greenhouse, pushing warm air up and out through roof vents.

The Davies Alpine House in London, England, uses biomimicry to recreate a mountainous habitat. Architects: Wilkinson Eyre Architects.

NATURE HAD IT FIRST

Architects are often asked to solve design problems. And after coming up with a solution to the problem, they sometimes discover that nature had the answer all along.

LIVING WITH WATER

If you lived in the Netherlands, you would have to learn to "live with water." A large part of the country is at or below sea level and, on average, there is a major flood every 12 years. Some architects are helping people in the Netherlands go with the flow by designing amphibious buildings that usually sit on dry land but can float if necessary.

Amphibious houses in Maasbommel, Netherlands, have foundations (bases) made of waterproof boxes that are filled with air and can float. Pairs of houses are fastened by sliding rings to a set of two steel posts that are anchored to the ground. When there is a flood, the houses rise with the water level without floating away. When the water goes down, the houses settle back on the land.

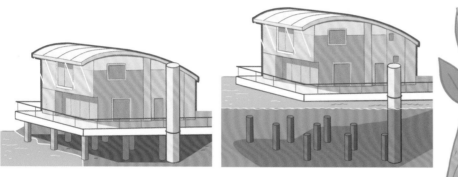

Amphibious houses in Maasbommel, Netherlands, rise and fall with the water levels. Architects: Factor Architecten.

A clever idea, BUT … nature came up with it first. The leaves of many aquatic plants, such as water lilies, have veins filled with air that help the leaves stay afloat. The plants also have very long petioles (stalks) rooted to the bottom of the pond. When the water rises, the petiole uncoils to allow the leaf to stay on the surface of the pond.

air chambers

A water lily's leaf has air chambers that help it float.

Meet the Architect:
Koen Olthuis

It's not surprising that Koen Olthuis became an aquatect — an architect who builds on water. His father is an architect and his mother comes from a long line of shipbuilders. Also, Olthuis lives in the Netherlands, a country that constantly battles rising seawaters.

But Olthuis chose to work *with* water, not fight against it. How? By building houses, apartment complexes and even whole city blocks that can float. Their unsinkable foundations are gigantic boxes filled with Styrofoam.

Olthuis is designing these structures as a way to deal with flooding, as well as sea levels that are rising due to climate change. He also sees his idea as a way of creating livable spaces in crowded cities.

But Olthuis's water-wise projects aren't all practical. He is also working on a floating hotel in Norway that looks like a snowflake, and a tourist attraction in the Maldives with a floating 18-hole golf course!

Warm It!

Do you know how your school is heated? If it uses a fossil fuel (a nonrenewable resource like coal, oil or gas), it's contributing to air pollution. Architects concerned about this are trying to design buildings that stay warm without harming the environment.

One of these architects is Rolf Disch, who decided to use solar energy to the max when he designed his own house. After all, using energy from the sun doesn't pollute and is free, too. He built an 18-sided house that can rotate 180 degrees. (That's like turning your head to look from your left shoulder over to your right shoulder.) A large solar panel on the roof rotates separately to capture the sun's rays throughout the day.

The reason Disch's house turns is because half of it has glass exterior walls, while the other half's exterior is made with wood. During the winter, the glass half of the house turns to follow the sun, absorbing heat (the way the inside of a car heats up in the sun). In the summer months, the insulated wooden side is turned toward the sun to shade the interior of the house and keep it cool.

Rolf Disch's house in Freiburg, Germany, is called the Heliotrope. In Greek, helios *means sun and* tropos *means turning toward or away from.*

It turns out that Arctic poppies take advantage of the sun's rays in a similar way. The cup-shaped flowers need to attract insects in order to reproduce. To do that, the poppies heat their centers by turning to face the sun as it moves across the sky. Insects are happy to warm up inside these mini solar satellite dishes while having a tasty meal. (During Arctic summers, when the sun never sets, the flowers rotate all day, every day.)

Sunflowers also track the sun. Scientists aren't sure why, but they think it might be to make the flowers more visible to insects or to speed up the formation of seeds. What scientists *do* know, though, is that it's definitely not for tanning!

The Arctic poppy tracks the sun as it moves across the sky.

Always Trust a Truss

A team of architects in Japan had a major challenge. They were asked to design a bridge that would take traffic from the mainland to the island where the Kansai International Airport was located. The bridge would have to be about 5 km (3 mi.) long. Normally, a suspension bridge would be used to span such a long distance. But being so close to an airport with all the planes taking off and landing, the tall towers and high roadway of a suspension bridge could be a disaster.

The Sky Gate Bridge R in Osaka, Japan, uses a truss pattern for support, similar to the metacarpal bones in a vulture's wing (below).

The solution? Build a truss bridge — a bridge that uses a triangular pattern for support. A truss bridge is low enough not to be in the way of low-flying airplanes. It's strong because of its use of triangles and it uses less material than other bridges, making it cheaper to build.

The result was the Sky Gate Bridge R, a double-decker truss bridge with lanes for cars on the upper level and tracks for trains on the lower level. The truss pattern used for this bridge is made of equilateral triangles (all three sides are the same length) with vertical supports.

BUT … nature was there first. Vultures have a pattern of equilateral triangles in their metacarpals. Your metacarpals are the bones in your hand from your knuckles to your wrist. A vulture's metacarpals are much longer than yours and are in their wings. Much like how triangles are used in a truss bridge, the pattern of bony triangles in a vulture's wings makes the wings strong, but still light, for flying.

Test a Truss

Try this activity to find out how strong and *truss*-worthy truss bridges really are.

You'll need:

modeling clay

two piles of books, about 20 cm (8 in.) high

two strips of Bristol board, each 15 cm x 30 cm (6 in. x 12 in.) long

1. Make 10 or more 2.5 cm (1 in.) balls of modeling clay (a little smaller than Ping-Pong balls).

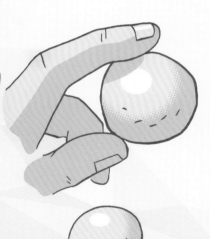

2. Stand the two piles of books 18 cm (7 in.) apart.

3. Place the two strips of Bristol board, one on top of the other, across the gap to form a bridge. How many balls do the strips hold?

4. Accordion-fold one of the strips lengthwise. Place it across the gap with the other (flat) strip on top. How many balls does your bridge hold now?

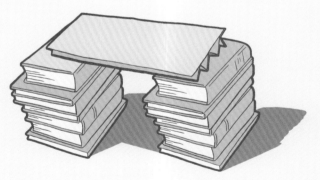

What happened?

When you used the accordion-folded strip with the flat strip, the triangles, or truss pattern, you created strengthened the bridge. This allows the bridge to support more weight without using more material.

THE NATURE OF NATURE

Just like people follow rules, so does nature. For example, nature recycles, uses a minimum of building materials, and makes curves and patterns. Some architects have been following these same rules when designing their structures.

Nature Recycles Everything

Nature doesn't need a garbage can because everything in the natural world can be recycled. For example, in the fall, the ground is covered with fallen leaves from trees — a feast for nature's recyclers. Worms, beetles, slugs and sow bugs chomp their way through all that leaf litter, breaking it down into tiny pieces. Microscopic organisms break them down further, releasing nutrients into the soil. In the spring, the nutrients are sucked up by tree roots, helping the trees grow new leaves.

Many architects are realizing that waste can actually be a resource. You might be surprised by the variety of recycled materials being used to make buildings and bridges!

Ship-Shape Buildings

Container City II in London, England, is a group of apartments that look something like a giant Lego set. It's actually just one example of how shipping containers — huge metal boxes used to transport goods across the ocean — are being recycled into homes and even schools around the world. After about 10 years of use, a shipping container is usually discarded, but some architects have realized that they are sturdy, are a cost-effective building material and can be arranged in lots of interesting combinations.

The Técnico Chixot Education Center in San Juan Comalapa, Guatemala, made ingenious use of old car and truck tires. Architects: Long Way Home.

A Tired School

Here's a trick question: When is a school tired? Answer: When its walls are made out of used car and truck *tires* packed with dirt.

The thick walls act as insulation, keeping the school in the town of San Juan Comalapa, Guatemala, cool during the day and preventing heat from escaping at night. To fill the gaps between the round tires, students were encouraged to collect used plastic bottles and stuff them with inorganic trash — garbage, such as plastic candy wrappers, that doesn't break down.

Container City II in London, England, is an example of large-scale recycling. Architects: Nicholas Lacey & Partners.

From Garbage to Gar-*bridge*

The Easter Dawyck Bridge in Scotland looks like an ordinary gray beam bridge. Driving over it, you'd probably never guess it was made of 50 tonnes (55 tons) of plastic that would otherwise have ended up in a landfill!

23

WASTE NOT, WANT NOT

Nature never uses more material than absolutely necessary. Check out these *bee*-utiful buildings that make the most of materials and space, much like honeybee hives do.

Beyond A, Bee, Cs

Most people's bedrooms have four walls, but for some university students at one college in Oxford, England, dorm rooms are six-sided hexagons. Architects designed these unusual dorms to make the most number of rooms fit on a small area of land. At the same time, the hexagonal shape still allows the individual rooms to be roomy.

Green Giants

When architects were asked to design the world's largest greenhouse, they were also instructed to use as few construction materials as possible so that there would be a minimum of waste. Impossible? Not if you use the hexagonal shape of honeycomb cells as a model.

The Eden Project building is made up of eight giant bubbles called biomes that are made mostly out of steel hexagons. The largest hexagon is 11 m (36 ft.) across — the height of a telephone pole. And amazingly, the steel structure weighs only slightly more than the air inside! By using hexagons, the architects were able to design strong structures using a minimum of materials with lots of space inside for plants.

The hexagonal rooms in the Beehive dorms in Oxford, England, make good use of a small amount of space. Architects: Architects' Co-Partnership.

The Eden Project in Cornwall, England, was also inspired by honeycomb cells. Architects: Grimshaw Architects.

A Sweet Deal

When building their honeycombs, honeybees create the most space with the least amount of material. How? By building the cells in their hives in the shape of hexagons. Try this activity to find out how it works.

You'll need:

thin wire, or three pipe cleaners 30 cm (12 in.) long

a ruler

scissors

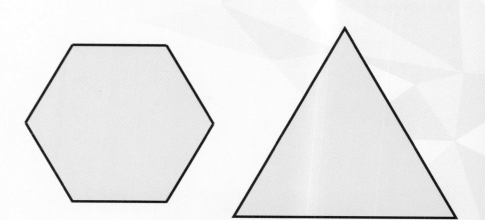

1. Measure the perimeter of (distance around) the first shape above. Starting at one corner, lay the wire along the sides until you come back to the starting point. Try to make sharp corners. Cut the wire where you stop.

What happened?

Even though all the shapes have the same area (space inside), you'll find that the hexagon has the shortest perimeter. This means it needs the least amount of wax to build. Also, with shared walls, less wax is needed when making more than one cell.

Saving on wax is a sweet deal for honeybees. Their abdominal glands produce the wax as tiny scales or flakes. Extracting, chewing and shaping the wax for a small nest takes about 66 000 bee hours. Whew, no wonder they use such an efficient shape!

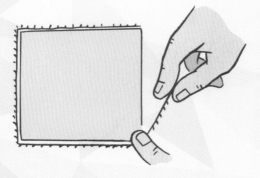

2. Straighten the wire and measure it.

3. Repeat for the other two shapes.

Nature's Curves

Have you ever thought about how curves are everywhere in nature — in winding rivers, rolling hills, flower petals, fish, eggs and nests, just to name a few examples. Psychologists have done tests that show people feel more comfortable looking at curved objects than at straight-edged, pointy ones. They believe this happens because curves are so often found in nature.

One architect who has taken this preference for curves to heart is Frank Gehry, whose famous curved buildings can be found all over the world. One of his best-known buildings is the Guggenheim Museum in Spain. Its rounded lines and shiny surface that seems to ripple as daylight changes have inspired its description as a "gargantuan bouquet of writhing silver fish." This is not such a surprising choice of words considering Gehry is fascinated by the movement and shape of fish.

The Guggenheim Museum in Bilbao, Spain, is covered with about 33 000 extremely thin titanium sheets that shimmer like giant fish scales. Architect: Frank Gehry.

• About 2000 years ago, the ancient Romans built aqueduct bridges to carry water across valleys to cities throughout the Roman Empire. One of the most famous is the Pont du Gard in southern France. It has three tiers, or levels, of arches that are the same shape but get smaller the higher up you go. And it's still standing today!

• When Gustave Eiffel designed his now-famous tower for the 1889 Paris World's Fair, his main challenge was to make sure that strong winds didn't topple it. In addition to building a wide base, he used open iron triangles in a variety of sizes to allow the wind to flow through.

• The city of Venice, Italy, has so many palaces with fractal structures, it's sometimes called "fractal Venice." The fractals can be seen in the palaces' many arches and windows. Some of them even have fractals in their floor patterns and chandeliers. One of the most beautiful palaces is Ca' d'Oro, which was built for a rich merchant between 1421 and 1431.

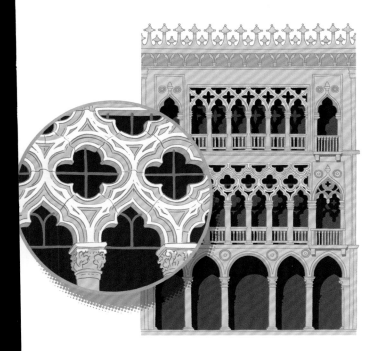

• Would you go to a mall to find fractals? You could if you lived in Addis Ababa, Ethiopia. The eight-story Lideta Mercato mall has patterns of squares on its facade created by open windows and colored glass. The architect was inspired by the colorful fractal patterns found on traditional Ethiopian dresses.

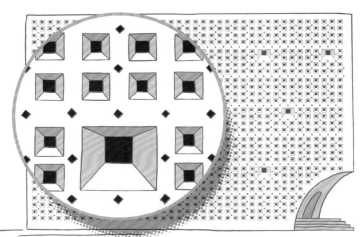

≡ IN HarmoNY WITH NaTURE ≡

You've probably heard of organic food, but what about organic architecture?
It grows out of nature, too — but in a different way. Before organic architects design
a building or bridge, they first look at the land that it will be on. Then they
create a design that will fit with the natural features of the land,
such as rivers, trees, rocks, hills and valleys.

Growing up in Toronto, Canada, Frank Gehry probably didn't realize time spent with his grandmother would influence his career. Together they built little houses and cities out of scraps of wood from the family's hardware store, and on Thursdays, they would get a live carp from the market for their Sabbath dinner. Frank loved the fish's shape and movements as it swam around in a bathtub filled with water.

Later, after Frank had become an architect, he saw some carp swimming in a pool in Japan. Their elegant shapes inspired him to eventually design curved buildings meant to show movement and inspire emotion.

A Frank Gehry design always starts as a model that he makes out of many different materials — pleated cardboard, paper-towel tubes and even pieces of an electric guitar. Once he is happy with his model, he uses a computer to create accurate drawings for his complicated structures.

Frank Gehry is not the only architect who designs buildings with curves. The Wave apartment complex in Vejle, Denmark, is located on a fjord — a narrow inlet from the sea between mountains. Its wavy pattern perfectly mirrors the water of the fjord as well as the surrounding hilly landscape.

The Wave apartment complex. Architects: Henning Larsen Architects.

NATURE'S PATTERNS

Have you ever noticed the patterns in nature? Next time you're outdoors, take a closer look at the stripes on caterpillars, the colors on butterfly wings and the web of an orb-spider. Once you start looking, you'll see patterns everywhere you go!

SHAPES WITHIN SHAPES WITHIN SHAPES

Many of nature's patterns are fractals. A fractal is made up of small parts that are identical in shape to the whole. For example, if you take broccoli apart, you can see that each part looks like a smaller version of the whole head. Fractal patterns are found throughout nature — in trees, mountains, leaves, flowers, seashells and even your lungs.

Architects have been using fractal patterns for centuries, although they didn't have a name for them. Then in the 1970s, mathematician Benoit Mandelbrot realized that natural objects have these special patterns, which he named "fractals." Since then, researchers have been discussing the reasons for their popularity in architecture. They realized that, in many cases, the use of fractals made buildings strong while using a minimum of materials. Researchers also think that the look of fractals is calming and pleasing to the eye because they mimic patterns seen in nature.

If you look around the world, you can find fractals in architecture everywhere!

Jellyfish: Some jellyfish have long stinging tentacles that hang down from a cup-shaped body. Many are bioluminescent, which means that their bodies produce their own light and can glow even in complete darkness.

Bird nest: Bird nests come in different shapes and are made of many kinds of materials. For example, some are built with grasses and strips of bark woven through softer materials and small twigs.

Durian fruit: Sharp spikes on the outside of this large, round fruit protect the one to seven large seeds inside its white flesh. Many people think the durian fruit is the smelliest fruit in the world, claiming it smells like old gym socks or rotting flesh.

THE REAL DEAL

Curious to see how some of the features of nature on pages 34 and 35 have been reflected in actual structures? Take a look.

The Lotus Building in Wujin, China. Architects: studio505.

It may look like a lotus flower floating on top of a lake, but the Lotus Building is actually a conference center attached to a two-story government building. The government building is underneath an artificial lake. How do you get to the Lotus Building? You walk through an underground tunnel from the land!

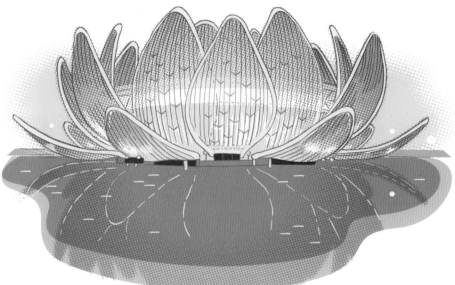

The World Birding Center in Mission, Texas. Architects: Lake/Flato Architects.

The curved metal roof on this birding center was designed to do what the leaves of agave desert plants do — collect as much water as possible in an arid environment. The grooves of the roof channel rainwater into pipes leading to giant water tanks. These tanks can store 177 914 L (47 000 gal.) of water at a time. That would fill an average-sized classroom!

The Scottish Exhibition and Conference Centre in Glasgow, Scotland. Architects: Foster + Partners.

This unique-looking building is a conference center with lots of exhibition space. It's easy to see why locals refer to it as "the armadillo." While its steel-covered roof can't curl up like an armadillo, its sections do act like a protective shell.

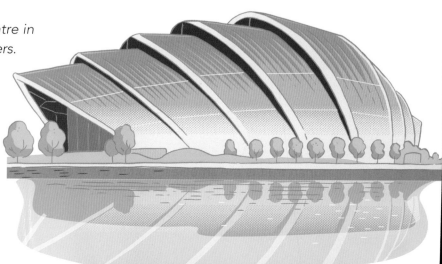

The Media-TIC building in Barcelona, Spain. Architects: Cloud 9.

This eco-friendly building has many features that save energy, including one inspired by the jellyfish. The metal parts of the main facade are painted with bioluminescent paint. During the day, the paint "charges" by absorbing energy from the sun. At night, this energy is released to give off a green glow.

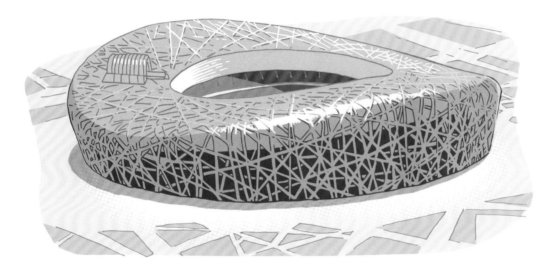

The Beijing National Stadium (a.k.a. The Bird's Nest) in Beijing, China. Architects: Jacques Herzog and Pierre de Meuron.

This enormous stadium built for the 2008 Olympic Games in Beijing, China, needed to be earthquake proof. When architects finished designing the web of twisting steel to give the stadium the strength it needed, they realized they had created a structure similar to a bird's nest, and the name stuck!

The Esplanade — Theatres on the Bay in Singapore. Architects: DP Architects.

Over 7000 movable triangular sunshades prevent this performing arts center in Singapore from overheating. It was nicknamed "the Durian" because it looks like the spiky tropical fruit, which grows in that part of the world.

THE FUTURE IS YOURS

If you're a creative person who likes to solve problems, maybe becoming an architect, designer or engineer is in your future. And if so, you might find yourself looking to nature for inspiration now that you know how it can hold the answers to so many design challenges. It could be something as awe-inspiring as a rainbow or as annoying as a mosquito or as tiny as a seed. Whatever it is, you'll need to figure out how it functions or works. If it's an animal, you can look at how it moves, how it eats and drinks, how it defends itself and even how it poops.

At the same time, you can look to nature for reminders of its rules — recycling, using a minimum of building materials, and using curves and patterns. And, of course, being aware of the beauty of nature, you'll want to make sure that your building or bridge fits in with the landscape where you'll be building it.

But even if you don't want to become an architect or engineer or designer, you can keep your eyes and imagination open for ideas in nature that might inspire you. You never know where that might lead!

GLOSSARY

abdominal: relating to the belly

amphibious: suitable for both land and water

architect: a person who designs buildings and bridges

architecture: the science and art of designing buildings and bridges

biome: a large area of the world sharing the same climate and plant life

biomimetic: imitating nature in a human-made object

cable: a strong, thick rope made of wires twisted together

condensation: a process in which water vapor changes from gas to liquid

dorm: short for *dormitory*, a building where students live

facade: the front or outside part of a building

fossil fuel: fuel found within the earth, such as coal, petroleum and natural gas

foundation: the base that supports a building

fractal: a pattern of small parts that are identical in shape to the whole

gherkin: a small cucumber used for making pickles

mast: a tall pole that supports a ship's sail

organic: having to do with nature

pollutant: a substance that makes air, water or soil unclean

saguaro cactus: a tall cactus with arms that grows in deserts in the southwestern United States

satellite dish: a bowl-shaped device used to receive signals from a satellite orbiting the earth

tentacle: a long, slender, flexible appendage used for feeling, holding or moving

truss bridge: a bridge that uses a triangular pattern for support

SOURCES

I used many resources when researching the information for this book. Some of them are:

Animal Architecture, by Ingo Arndt. New York: Harry N. Abrams, 2014.

Architecture: Nature, by Philip Jodidio. Munich: Prestel, 2006.

Architecture Follows Nature: Biomimetic Principles for Innovative Design, by Ilaria Mazzoleni. Boca Raton: CRC Press, 2013.

The Biology of the Honey Bee, by Mark L. Winston. Cambridge: Harvard University Press, 1987.

Biomimicry: Innovation Inspired by Nature, by Janine M. Benyus. New York: HarperCollins, 2002.

Biomimicry in Architecture, by Michael Pawlyn. London: RIBA Publications, 2011.

The Biomimicry Institute. www.biomimicry.org.

Built by Animals: The Natural History of Animal Architecture, by Mike Hansell. Don Mills: Oxford University Press, 2007.

Eco Structures: Forms of Sustainable Architecture, by Sabrina Leone and Leone Spita. Edited by Gianpaola Spirito. Vercelli: White Star, 2009.

Inspired by Nature Animals: The Building/Biology Connection, by Alejandro Bahamón and Patricia Pérez. New York: W.W. Norton & Company, 2009.

Inspired by Nature Plants: The Building/Botany Connection, by Alejandro Bahamón, Patricia Pérez and Alex Campello. New York: W.W. Norton & Company, 2008.

Sources You Might Enjoy

Biomimicry: Inventions Inspired by Nature, by Dora Lee. Toronto: Kids Can Press, 2011.

From Mud Huts to Skyscrapers: Architecture for Children, by Christine Paxmann. Munich: Prestel, 2012.

INDEX